MW01394013

Why I Love My
HORSE

101 Dang Good Reasons

Ellen Patrick

Why I Love My Horse

Copyright © 2006 Sweetwater Press

ISBN-13: 978-1-58173-647-2
ISBN-10: 1-58173-647-9

Jacket and text design by Miles G. Parsons
Printed in Italy

1. Biggest heart in the world.

2. Best listener in the world.

—ᦙᦙ—

3. World-champion snacker.

4. Did I say world-champion snacker?

5. Wrote the book on how to roll on your back (also known as ruining a good bath).

6. Bottomless brown eyes hold all the answers.

7. Those eyelashes!

---~~~---

8. Holds a master's degree in patience.

9. Holds a master's degree in friendship.

—⦿—

10. Holds a Ph.D. in loyalty.

11. Always understands.

12. Always forgives.

13. Always lets me
know I did something
to be forgiven.

14. Knows what I'm thinking before I do.

15. Has a secret smile reserved just for me.

—〰—

16. Always ready for company.

17. Always ready to play.

—◊◊◊—

18. A genius at finding sneaky ways to get a treat.

19. Knows all my secrets.

20. Knows how to use my secrets against me.

21. Taught me who I really am (and who I'm not).

———ᴍ———

22. Puts the wind in my hair.

26. Doesn't care what I look like.

27. Doesn't care what my hair looks like.

—ɯ—

28. Doesn't care what kind of car I drive.

29. Only cares whether I have a peppermint.

30. When we're riding we own the world.

31. No one can stop us.

—⁂—

32. No one can defeat us.

33. We have an unbreakable bond. (Our bones, however, are breakable.)

34. Wrote the book on running, jumping, and playing.

—⦿—

35. Knows the importance of pasture-mates.

36. Those great big sighs.

37. That prickly chin.

—⁓—

38. That amazing ability to outrun my troubles.

39. Your mystery.

40. Your fear of ghosties.

41. Your sense of humor.

—⁂—

42. Your compassion.

43. Your warmth.

44. Your steamy breath (yuck).

45. Your slobbery kisses (double yuck).

46. That grunching sound you make when you eat.

47. Ears have a language all their own.

48. Your love of company.

—⁂—

49. The way you rub your nose on me.

50. The way you butt me with your head.

—⦚—

51. The way you sleep standing up.

52. The way you sleep lying down.

53. The way you're always happy to see me.

54. How good my muscles hurt after a ride.

—⁓—

55. Taught me never to give up.

56. Taught me to climb back on.

—∽—

57. Taught me the true meaning of carrots.

58. Pretty much trained me from the ground up.

59. Does double duty as a fence demolition expert.

60. Does double duty as a mattress.

—✺—

61. Does double duty as a flying machine.

62. Has numerous mysterious interpretations of the word "go."

63. Affords the perfect excuse to spend all my money on horse stuff.

64. Never stops amazing with variety of bit slobber.

65. Is the perfect audience for bridle cleaning, stall mucking, and many otherwise uninteresting pastimes.

66. Goes through more new shoes than Imelda Marcos.

67. Can find anything, in any pocket.

68. Expert on all the ways to eat an apple.

69. Black strap molasses, anyone?

70. Sugar, anyone?

—⁂—

71. Small items not normally considered digestible, anyone?

72. One hundred percent effective in eliminating loneliness.

73. One hundred percent effective in eliminating boredom.

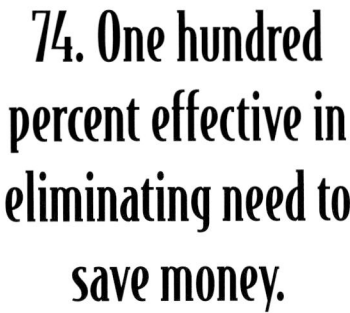

74. One hundred percent effective in eliminating need to save money.

75. Can do tricks. Sort of.

—∞—

76. Never lets me forget I'm the boss (ha ha).

77. Understands that cleanliness is just not natural.

78. Smart.

---ᗡ⎯

79. Funny.

---ᗡ⎯

80. Honest.

81. Loving.

—~~~—

82. Sneaky.

—~~~—

83. Opinionated.

84. Compassionate.

85. Affectionate.

86. Natural-born therapist.

87. Natural-born food connoisseur.

88. Natural-born
con artist.

—⁂—

89. Natural-born
friend.

90. Wrote the book on trust.

—⁕—

91. Wrote the book on companionship.

92. Wrote the book on nuzzling.

93. Wrote the book on practical jokes.

94. Wrote the book on avoiding entering a trailer.

—⁓—

95. Wrote a book called <u>Putting Things in Perspective</u>.

96. Takes care of me in ways no human ever could.

97. Has a soul as big as Texas.

—ⱳⱳ—

98. This is the only transportation I'll ever really need.

99. This may be the only friend I'll ever really need.

100. This may be my very best friend in the world.

101. Out of all the humans on earth, my horse picked me.